Happy Birthday Meatball Love, Spaghetti

Written by
BRIAN BECK

Copyright © 2025 by Brian Beck
Illustrations © Copyright 2025 Brian Beck

Book Design by Sketco Studio

All rights reserved.

Library of Congress No. 2025918593

ISBN: 978-1-952991-52-3

BROOKLYN WRITERS PRESS
An imprint of Book Biz Hub, LLC

brooklynwriterspress.com

Meatball woke up so excited,
"Ready or not, here I come!"

It was his birthday, and he knew that meant
playing the annual birthday hide-and-seek
with his best friend Spaghetti,
the chicken.

Psst, hey you!
This year I could use your help to guide
Meatball through the alphabet to find me.

Just one thing, if you spot me hiding, shh—don't tell Meatball, let's keep it a surprise.

Anchovy

Starting with the letter A, Meatball *hooked* up with **Ann Chové**, a French chef and the *best cook* he knew.

When Meatball couldn't find Spaghetti, he said "Hmmm something is fishy around here!"
"*Can it!*" Ann said.

Meatball yelled to Frizz the **Bee** as he was gliding back and forth,

"Have you heard any **buzz** about Spaghetti?" Frizz Bee smiled and said,

"Oh honey, you know that even if I knew, it's none of your *beeswax!*"

Clownfish

Giggles the Clownfish, one of Meatball's funniest friends, video called to wish him a happy birthday.

Meatball told Giggles about his Mommy kicking him in her sleep.

"Meatball said, Keep your distance—at least two feet!" Meatball barked with laughter. "Ya know... two feet?!"

Deer

Spaghetti loves to dance, so Meatball went to the club to see his deerest friend, DJ Rudy.

Meatball didn't find Spaghetti and couldn't hear very well over the music so he used sign language:

If anybody *nose* where Spaghetti is, it would be his friend **Ellie Phant**, the magician, Meatball thought.

Elephant

Meatball was amazed watching Ellie pull poop emojis, the letter Es, and pasta out of her trunk, but none of them were Spaghetti, so Meatball performed his own magic trick and disappeared.

Meatball reappeared in the park and heard Butter, Fire, and Thyme Flies chatting.

He tried to ask about Spaghetti, but they **NEVER** stopped talking.

Giggling, Meatball told the flies to "Zip-it!"

Fly

Giraffe

Meatball called Guppy the Giraffe, someone who is willing to stick his neck out for friends.

Meatball kept asking about Spaghetti until Guppy shouted, "You're a real pain in my neck!"

Meatball received a helpful tip about hiding spots from Horace the Horse, a private detective who spoke in a deep, scratchy voice.

Meatball wanted to help him too, so he poured him tea with honey and said, "This is so you don't sound so.... hoarse!" "Get it? Hoarse, horse?"

Meatball laughed, cracking himself up.

Horse

Irish Doodle

Horace gave him a tip then asked Macaroni the Pony to take Meatball to Yankee Stadium to ask the Irish Doodles for advice.

There were no signs of Spaghetti, so Meatball offered the Irish Doodles a ride home on Macaroni.

Then...the Yankee Doodles went to town, riding on their pony.

Meatball needed a new ride, so he went to get a Jaguar. Jerilyn the Jaguar was playing cards with **Bob the Bobcat, Ant Joyce,** and **Larry the Leopard**, who was wearing a hat and sunglasses.

When Meatball saw Larry the Leopard pull cards from his hat he shouted,

"You're a Cheetah!"

Jaguar

King Crab

K was next, so Meatball went to see His Highness, **Cake the King Crab**.

Cake grumbled that he hadn't seen Spaghetti and snapped. "Go bother someone else—I'm in a pinch!"

Meatball didn't like His Majesty being so snippy, so he barked, "Stop being such a **crumby crab, Cake!**"

Lion

Meatball saw Linda the Lion, lying on a rock. She was known for making up stories.

"I just saw Spaghetti get into a spaceship and fly to outer space!" Linda said with a smirk.

"You're a *lying* lying lion!" Meatball said.

Macaw

Meatball went to see the all-knowing fourteen-year-old, **Aubrey the Macaw**, a Parrot Card Reader.

Meatball asked, "Have you seen Spaghetti?"

Aubrey the Macaw replied, "Squawk, have you seen Spaghetti?" It quickly turned into a parroty!

N for Gnat, Meatball chuckled, remembering his classmate's bakery, *Doh!*

Nat was an amazing baker, but a terrible speller—he always came in last at every spelling bee.

Since Spaghetti loves sweets, Meatball went to see if she was hiding there.

Nat hadn't seen Spaghetti, but he baked Meatball a yummy birthday *browknee!*

Owl

Meatball met *with his very wise friend,* Thurston Owl III, before he went on a three-hour boat tour.

Meatball: "Have you seen Spaghetti?"
Thurston Owl III: "Who?"

That's when Meatball knew something was *afowl.*

Meatball tiptoed behind PopPop the Panda before yelling "Bam-BOO!"

There was a *pandamonium* of giggles!

PopPop hadn't seen Spaghetti, but he was so excited to see Meatball he gave him the biggest *birthday bear-hug!*

Quahog

Meatball went to the Southy Smaat Spaa
to meet Lynn Guine (pronounced "Gweenie")
a Quahog clam who loved soaking
in the hot tub.

Meatball tried to ask about Spaghetti but was
interrupted when Lynn Guine yelled out:

"NAWT TOO HAWT!"

Meatball went to pick the brain of Sir Jin the Rhino, a British artist who invented a type of plaster for sculpting known as Rhino-plasty.

Sir Jin could scents that Spaghetti was up to something special, but couldn't tell Meatball.

Rhino

Sloth

Meatball skedaddled to meet Moe the Sloth for a birthday snack.

They were having a great time, but Moe kept asking the waiter,

"Can. You. Re. Heat. My. Alphabet. Soup?"

Finally, on the nineteenth request, Meatball said "Bro! You're a slow Moe!"

Meatball was late to meet **Myrtle the Turtle**, a famous winter clothes designer who is iconic for her *high-neck sweaters*.

Myrtle had not seen Spaghetti, but they had a blast shopping for neckties for Myrtle's boxing brothers, **Cuff and Link Balboa**.

Turtle

Unicorn

Meatball needed some luck, and what's luckier than a uni-corn?

He went to the cornfield, plucked a single kernel from a cob and held it up. "Uni-corn, am I close to finding Spaghetti?" he asked. Nothing happened.

More like U for uncooperative, Meatball thought with a smirk.

Meatball went to Mets Stadium to meet **Dee Racula, the Vampire Bat.**

He didn't find any clues about Spaghetti, but he did hit **a fang-tastic home run!**

Vampire Bat

Maybe Spaghetti is hiding by Worm the Jeweler, Meatball thought.

He didn't find Spaghetti there either, but he bought a beautiful diamond pinky ringworm so he could look like his Daddy, Matzah Ball!

Worm

AXolotl

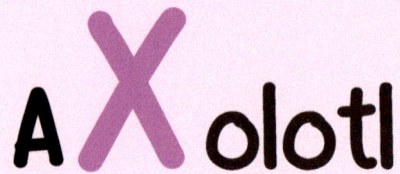

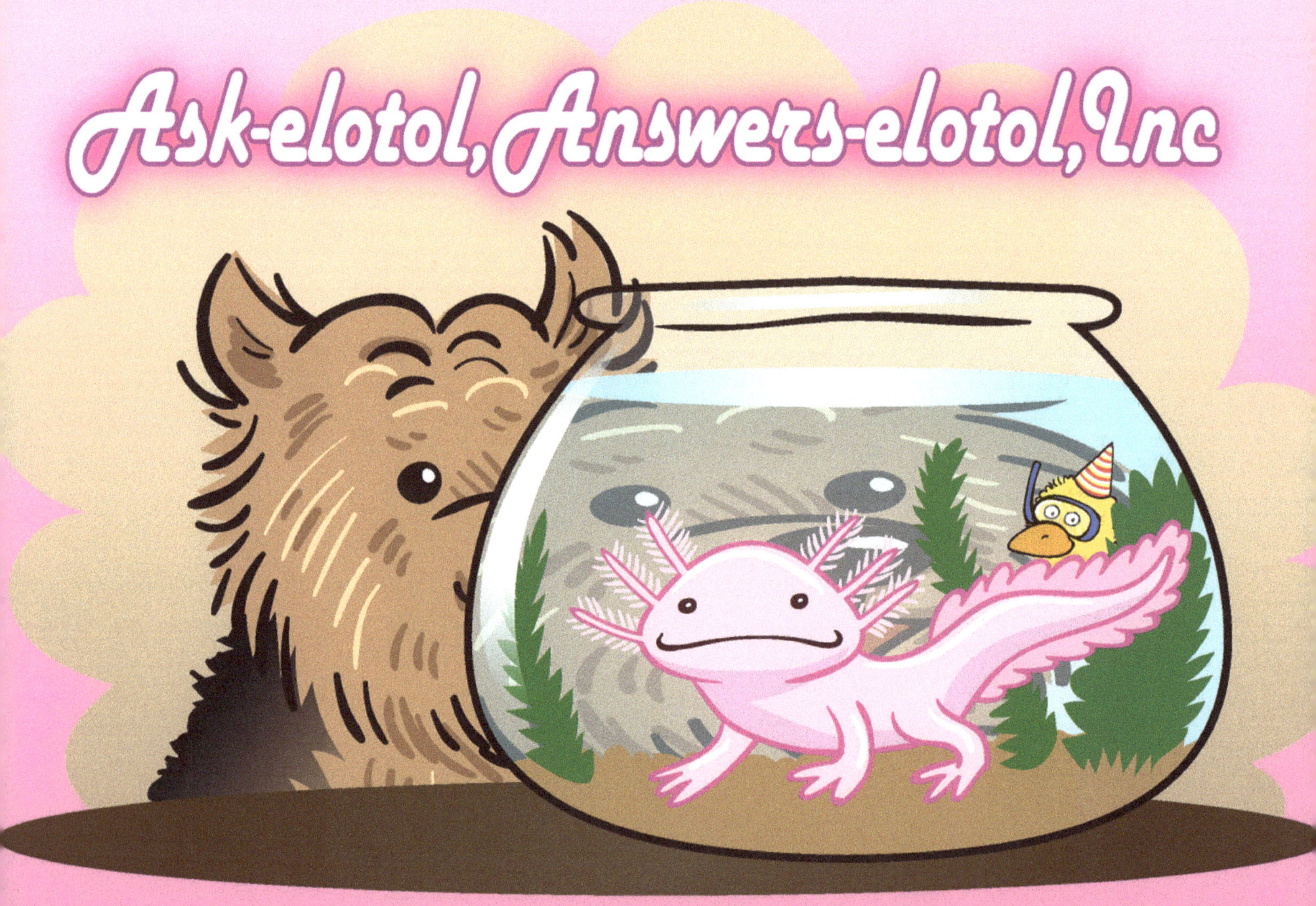
Ask-elotol, Answers-elotol, Inc

Meatball went to see Mckennolotl the Axolotl at "Ask-elotol, Answers-elotol, Inc."

"Do you know why I'm coming up dry on Spaghetti?" Meatball asked.

Mckennolotl gave a big wink and said, "You need to see someone who's got the sauce!"

Meatball's eyes lit up.
"Of course—my Mommy!"

Y for Yorkie "Hey, that's me!
And who knows me better than me?
My mommy!"

Meatball jumped into his mommy's arms, where he fit perfectly.
He stretched, and his mommy said,
"BIG stretch, Meatball!
I'm so proud of you for knowing the whole alphabet," before giving him a bunch of birthday kisses.

"Thank you, Mommy.
I think I know where Spaghetti is hiding!"

Yorkie

Zorse

Meatball called out for his zany Aunt Zodi the Zorse, who arrived in a zippy. Meatball jumped on, and they zoomed off to his favorite restaurant, Woofgang's.

When Meatball walked in,
he was met with the loudest,
"SURPRISE!!!"

Spaghetti gave him the most
thoughtful gift, to be surrounded
by the ones he loves most—his mommy,
daddy, family and friends, and most of all,
YOU!

(Psst. Want to join Meatball's surprise party?
Ask a grown-up to help you add your photo on the opposite
page—so you're part of the fun, too!)

"Happy Birthday Meatball!"
Love, Spaghetti.

Want More Meatball & Spaghetti Fun?

Scan the QR code to discover:
Bonus activities and games, coloring pages
featuring the duo and sneak peeks at
upcoming adventures.

Fun surprises just for you!
Ask a grown-up to help you scan
the QR code with their
phone or tablet.

meatballandspaghetti.com

instagram | facebook
@_meatballandspaghetti_

Dedicated to my Mommy
for loving me and taking care of me
and cleaning my doodie.

And to my little sisters, Aubrey and
Mckenna, thank you for helping with this book and all the
fun we had during our bedtime antics. Goodnight!

Love,
Meatball

About the Author

Brian Beck is a healthcare executive and former stand-up comedian who discovered his best material is at home with his wife and daughters. His co-author, Meatball, is a 7-pound toy Yorkie with big ideas and an even bigger attitude. Though Brian thinks he wrote this book, Meatball was really calling the shots—Brian just handled the typing. Together, they created this ABC adventure for the whole family. Stay tuned for more!

About the Illustrator

Ho Lie John is an Indonesian character designer and illustrator known for his playful and humorous approach to visual storytelling. His quirky characters make people smile through vibrant colors, light-hearted themes, and exaggerated personalities. He shares his sketches, concept art, and daily inspirations on Instagram @holejohn

Thank You for Reading
Happy Birthday Meatball, Love Spaghetti
An ABC Adventure

We hope you had a paw-some time learning your ABCs with Meatball and his favorite toy, Spaghetti!

Did this book make you laugh?

We'd love to hear about it. Ask a grown-up to help you leave a review and tell other families about your adventure.

This is just the beginning!
Meatball and Spaghetti have more exciting adventures waiting for you.

Happy reading, little adventurers!

♥ The Brooklyn Writers Press

BROOKLYN
WRITERS PRESS

www.ingramcontent.com/pod-product-compliance
Lightning Source LLC
Chambersburg PA
CBHW040001290426
43673CB00077B/293